W9-BCA-662

The Inner Beauty Series
Defining Your Worth in the Eyes of God

PUT AWAY
Your Past

Charisma
HOUSE
Books about Spirit-Led Living

Lisa Bevere

Put Away Your Past by Lisa Bevere
Published by Charisma House
A part of Strang Communications Company
600 Rinehart Road
Lake Mary, Florida 32746
www.charismahouse.com

Unless otherwise noted, all Scripture quotations are from the Holy Bible, New International Version. Copyright © 1973, 1978, 1984, International Bible Society. Used by permission.

Scripture quotations marked NKJV are from the New King James Version of the Bible. Copyright © 1979, 1980, 1982 by Thomas Nelson, Inc., publishers. Used by permission.

Cover design by Rachel Campbell

Library of Congress Catalog Card Number: 2001099920
International Standard Book Number: 0-88419-840-5

02 03 04 05   87654321
Printed in the United States of America

Contents

Introduction   v

1   Put Away Worldly Comparisons   1

2   Fear: The Battle for Your Mind   27

3   Awake, Daughter of Zion   51

4   Rise Up From the Dust   59

5   Your Past Is Not Your Future   69

Conclusion   83

Introduction

Just as a young woman spends hours preparing herself for her wedding—visiting the hairstylist, getting a facial, having her makeup professionally applied and putting on her beautiful bridal gown, so too we must prepare our spiritual lives to be ready to radiate the inner beauty of the woman of God we were created to be.

An important part of the preparation is clearing our lives of the past. We cannot turn fully into the beautiful future God has for us until we completely turn away from our past. In this second book in the Inner Beauty Series we will learn how to move away from the hindering factors of our past so that we can radiate the inner beauty of our hearts.

We are a people in transition. We all have areas in our lives we are afraid to entrust even to God's care. We must learn to release our past to God.

Like children who bring their broken toys to a parent to fix, we must bring our broken lives to God, yielding them completely to His control. As the old preacher said, we must "let go and let God!"

> We cannot turn fully into
> the beautiful future God has
> for us until we completely
> turn away from our past.

I like to compare letting go with the process of learning to swim. It can be both exhilarating and terrifying. In order to swim you must first learn to float, allowing the water to hold you up. Only then do you discover the freedom and liberty of swimming. This natural principle reflects a spiritual transition from our natural rule to the rule of the Holy Spirit.

Paul learned to do this. And he left us an example to follow:

> I do not consider myself yet to have taken

hold of it. But one thing I do: Forgetting what is behind and straining toward what is ahead, I press on toward the goal to win the prize for which God has called me heavenward in Christ Jesus.

—PHILIPPIANS 3:13

For the woman of God, the prize is the radiant inner beauty of a life that reflects the very heart of God.

Adapted from Lisa Bevere, *Out of Control and Loving It!*, 15–16.

BEAUTY TIP

WE CAN ONLY RIGHTLY DIVIDE

TRUTH WHEN WE HAVE

FIRST APPLIED IT TO OUR

OWN HEARTS.

Put Away Worldly Comparisons

Do not judge, or you too will be judged. For in the same way you judge others, you will be judged, and with the measure you use, it will be measured to you.

—Matthew 7:1–2

n order to put away our past successfully, we must learn to quit making judgmental, worldly comparisons to others. Honesty and truth will always outlive lies. This world's standards are lies. There are true standards of measurement in God's kingdom. They may not be measured in actual inches or centimeters, but definite units of measure nevertheless exist. The incremental size of such units does not matter; God uses units of measure to designate His proportional return to us.

We will see this theme repeated time and again in God's Word. We cannot judge truth until we know and apply truth to ourselves. Without a clear and accurate perspective, we will not recognize the truth when it presents itself. It is imperative that we first remove any obstructions that may bar us from the truth. We are warned:

> Do not judge, or you too will be judged.
> For in the same way you judge others, you
> will be judged, and with the measure you
> use, it will be measured to you.
> —MATTHEW 7:1–2

If we judge, we will be judged. This is a spiritual principle. One day while drying my hair, I was mentally judging a friend who had hurt me. I told myself, *I always knew she was this way. I'm staying away from her!*

If we judge, we will be judged.

This person had repeatedly hurt me. Over the years I had flitted in and out of a friendship with her. One minute we were the best of friends, the next enemies without any apparent cause for the shift in sentiment. Then she would float back into a relationship with me, only to have the cycle play itself out again later. Gossip was inevitably involved, and I decided I was finally through with her!

After making this determination, I expected to feel freedom but instead I felt grieved as the Spirit checked me. I defended my position: "I'm *right* to judge her; she *is* this way!"

God, the Only Judge

Immediately, I sensed the Spirit of God question me. "Is that what you want Me to say about you?"

I was stunned; after all, *I* wasn't the issue here! What did *I* have to do with this? *I* was talking about *her*. The Holy Spirit continued, "When you judge someone you are saying they are never going to change and therefore you don't have to be reconciled with them. If you judge them, then I must judge you. Do you want Me to say, 'Lisa is never going to change'?"

3

I thought about it. I knew that on the Day of Judgment God would look at one group and, in essence, say, "Though I've given you a chance time and time again to repent, you never have. You are never going to change. Therefore, there is no reconciliation for you." This group of people would then be told to depart eternally from His presence.

> God could see in a dimension unknown to man because He sees into the unseen, unspoken treasuries of our hearts.

I knew that God would also judge the other group, His sheep, because He knew they would never change either, that they would always love Him and stay faithful to Him. God could see in a dimension unknown to man because He sees into the unseen, unspoken treasuries of our hearts.

There is only one Lawgiver and Judge, the

one who is able to save and destroy. But
you—who are you to judge your neighbor?
—James 4:12

I had presumed to know someone else's heart,
and when I judged this person I was grieved
because I was placing myself under judgment.
God alone is judge and He will share this position
with no one. I knew this young woman's actions,
but I could only guess at her motives.

Although I thought my information was accurate, it was at best incomplete. It is important to
note that this conversation never hit the airwaves;
it took place only in my head. I never intended to
publicly denounce her, but I had pronounced her
guilty as prosecutor and judge in the biased court
of my heart.

It is possible to be right
and wrong.

Now that I had seen the truth, I wanted to
repent. But I was concerned that my repentance

might lead me back into an unhealthy relationship with her. Before praying, I protested, "God, it's true! This cycle keeps happening."

The Holy Spirit gently encouraged me, "I did not say you have to fellowship with her or that your assessment was totally in correct—only that your reaction to it is wrong."

Partly Right, Partly Wrong

It was then that I realized it is possible to be right *and* wrong. I needed to separate this woman's actions from her motives. It was within reason to decide that her *actions* warranted my caution in all future interactions. I would need to exercise God's wisdom in my relationship with her. But I was not to set myself up as judge over her.

> Because judgment without mercy will be shown to anyone who has not been merciful. Mercy triumphs over judgment!
> —James 2:13

My judgment had been harsh, not allowing for any recourse or repentance on her part. I had forgotten that the measure or amount I had apportioned for her judgment was the same measure, manner, or proportion God would choose when He portioned mine. I have come to this realization—that though I *deserve* judgment, I *need* mercy. If I want mercy, I must therefore be merciful, because only mercy triumphs over judgment.

We receive God's mercy not because we deserve it but because, in Christ, mercy always triumphs!

> Why do you look at the speck of sawdust in your brother's eye and pay no attention to the plank in your own eye? How can you say to your brother, "Let me take the speck out of your eye," when all the time there is a plank in your own eye? You hypocrite, first take the plank out of your own eye, and then you will see clearly to remove the speck from your brother's eye.
>
> —MATTHEW 7:3–5

I probably had enough planks in my eyes to build an entertainment center. My most prominent plank was a tendency to be critical and to judge, while this woman's speck was a tendency to gossip.

The scripture in Matthew 7:3–5 must be interpreted in context with the preceding scripture in verses 1–2: *Do not judge, or you too will be judged.* A speck may blur your vision but a plank obstructs it, and judging others is a plank.

"Plank" Vision

Such planks become all you see. People with "plank" vision find that everywhere they look, they see only the flaws of others. Sawdust is the by-product of construction with such wood planks. The sawdust of others becomes the focus. Those with "plank" vision recognize in others a by-product of themselves.

> If I want mercy, I must therefore be merciful, because only mercy triumphs over judgment.

Sawdust is not as obvious as specks or planks. People with planks walk about, totally unaware of their own blinders, all the while attempting to remove the various specks from the eyes of others. When you get a mental picture of it, you will see how silly and dangerous it is to think any of us can help anyone else while there are so many planks protruding from our own eyes. None of us would go to a blindfolded surgeon, now would we?

Those with "plank" vision recognize in others a by-product of themselves.

Our purpose is not to judge others with the truths we learn, but to judge ourselves. So often it is easier to listen to the sermon and apply it to someone next to us. Or to read a book for someone else. I have done it…I know. I'll read a book and think, *This is great! Boy, I know some people who really need to read this!*

My mind begins to race as I scheme how I'll get each person a copy of the book or how I'll find a way to read passages of it out loud to them.

Now that's all right if I just want to share something that has *already* helped me.

When the planks in our own eyes are removed, we will be able to see clearly again and our motives will be pure.

The only problem is I usually skip the "helped me" step and leap right into the process of helping or changing others. I become so busy reading the book for others that I fail to apply its truths to my own life. It is all right to help another when our eyes are clear. Jesus said first remove the plank from our own eye, then take care of the speck in our brother's eye. When the planks in our own eyes are removed, we will be able to see clearly again and our motives will be pure.

HOW DO WE COMPARE?

We can only rightly divide truth when we have first applied it to our own hearts. For too long we have not had accurate information by which to measure ourselves. We have assessed ourselves by those around us and by our own past failures and successes. God does not measure us this way. Paul warns us:

> We do not dare to classify or compare ourselves with some who commend themselves. When they measure themselves by themselves and compare themselves with themselves, they are not wise.
>
> —2 Corinthians 10:12

Paul was pretty bold, and if he says he wouldn't dare to do something, then it is definitely something we also need to avoid. Yet, often we have a tendency to compare ourselves with others. Our reasoning goes something like this: *Well, I do more than Sally does! She only has one child and doesn't even sing in the choir!* or, *I don't gossip like Susie, that girl is never off the phone!* These exchanges may temporarily ease our consciences. Though it may be true, Sally and Susie are *not* God's standard for our lives. God says this line of reasoning and justification is not wise.

He wants us to have a head-on collision with

11

truth, not with someone in the choir loft. I have learned that when I am confronted with truth, it is best not to defend myself but to submit to it. Hidden in the initial pain of impact is the power to rise from my captivity.

> When the truth of God's
> Word is applied, we can
> see with our eyes,
> hear with our ears, and
> know with our hearts.

Deception comes in when we resist truth. In a confrontation with truth, reasoning and justifying ourselves will lead straight into deception. When the truth of God's Word is applied, we can see with our eyes, hear with our ears, and know with our hearts.

Since we are dealing with the topic of putting away our past, truth will be our constant companion. Unless we deal with every hindering factor from the past, we will still be weighted down, unable to step freely and unencumbered into the destiny God has in our future. It is time to strike the balance between truth and worth. Proverbs 11:1 tells us:

> The LORD abhors dishonest scales, but accurate weights are his delight.

God hates dishonest or unjust measurements. He delights in honest, just, and fair ones. Women have been measured by dishonest scales for far too long.

WEIGHTS AND MEASURES

A scale is the unit that measures weight or a rate of exchange, matching value for value and worth for worth. For example, if a dollar buys a fourth of a pound of jelly beans, you would place a quarter-pound weight on one side of the scale and add jelly beans to the other side until both sides balanced.

An honest scale is a symbol of justice, representing equality, equity and fairness. When a scale is balanced it is considered to be just. When a scale of justice is unbalanced, it has been tipped unfairly in one direction by influence or deceptive weights. Its calculations are no longer trustworthy.

We have all heard the term, "worth its weight in gold." This saying has its origins in ancient times, when valuables were placed on just such a scale and weighed in proportion to an identical measure of purest gold.

In order to try this form of measure today, you would first determine the exact weight of the item in question, then place an accurate representation of this weight on one side of the scale and place gold on the other side until both balanced. Pound for pound, the value of the item being weighed could be proven equal to that of gold.

> God is exposing a practice
> that has been conducted
> in secret, today and
> throughout the centuries.

I believe Proverbs 11:1 has both a practical and a spiritual application. To better understand the spiritual application we must first gain a good understanding of its natural application. In the practical sense, this scripture refers to *dishonest scales*, which describe the fraudulent selling and buying by use of scales or balances. God is exposing a practice that has been conducted in secret, today and throughout the centuries.

Vendors would tinker with scales and misrepresent weights to take advantage of their customers. For example, if you were to request one pound of flour from a dishonest vendor, he would place the lightened version of a one-pound weight on one side of the scale and your flour on the other side.

As you watched, he would add or deduct flour until the scales appeared to balance. Your flour would be transferred into a sack or container and you'd be sent on your way. As you walked away, you would have no way of knowing that your sack was shy a few ounces of flour.

You would have been certain the measure of it was accurate. After all, you watched just to make sure—but the merchant's one-pound balance weight actually weighed just fourteen ounces. You paid for more flour than you received.

In this manner, merchants were able to increase their profit margin. When you went home and dumped what you thought was a pound of flour into your recipe for bread, you found out there was a problem. The only way to avoid this sort of theft was to go to a reputable source and make accurate weights of your own. But even using your own weights, the merchants would argue that their weights were right and yours were too heavy.

Deceitful Gain

Merchants also used this practice when they purchased grain from farmers. For their suppliers they had another set of weights. These weights were heavier than what they actually represented. For example, a one-pound weight might really weigh eighteen ounces. Farmers would sell their grain to the merchants to market, usually in large quantities. A measure that was off just a little would mean great profit to the merchant—and great but unknown loss to the farmer.

If a farmer brought in one hundred pounds of grain, he had no way of knowing its weight because he had no scales. This put him in the position of having to trust the justice of the merchant's scale. If the merchant said his hundred pounds of wheat weighed only ninety-five pounds, the farmer accepted it.

Thus the merchant had received a bonus five pounds. If ten farmers came to him with a hundred pounds of grain each, at the close of the day this dishonest merchant would have acquired fifty pounds of grain for which he never paid. He would turn around and sell it for more than what it was worth.

In ancient times, the only way to avoid this sort of deception was to have your own method of weighing your goods before you brought them to market.

> If you don't have any accurate appraisal of your worth, you will sell out for far less.

This theft was not limited to small units of measure and purchases but encompassed sales with all units of measurement. Though practiced in secret, God warned against it in Leviticus 19:35:

> Do not use dishonest standards when measuring length, weight or quantity.

This form of dishonesty had been used to move ancestral boundary lines, rob farmers and cheat consumers. God wanted His children to be protected from this treachery. His people had naively trusted the dishonest merchants for too long. After the Lord's warning, measures were taken to protect consumers and suppliers from such dishonest trade. Accurate and standardized weights were established.

It is no different today. If you do not have an accurate weight of measurement, you will probably receive far less than what you paid for. If you don't have any accurate appraisal of your worth, you will sell out for far less.

Dishonest weights will also cause you to sell yourself short. Like the farmer, you will have been cheated. Or like a consumer, you will go through life thinking you are purchasing a pound, when you have actually been shortchanged. If you accept the merchant's measure, or value, as accurate you will never know you've been undersold.

Our search is for an accurate measure, one that balances truth *and* worth.

To counteract this deception, we will need to go to an honest source and get some accurate measuring weights, ones that have not been tampered with or hollowed out by the merchants of this world. Our search is for an accurate measure, one that balances truth *and* worth. It must be pure, incorruptible, solid and tested. There is only one source to find this type of measure. It is found in the treasury of God's counsel and wisdom. Once we find this measure, we must use it to assure that we will never again be sold something less valuable.

This measure will consist of truth. For it is *God's truth* that sets us free. Let's pattern our quest for truth after Solomon's search. Although he was the wisest man ever to live, he was the first to admit he did not hold within himself the answers. Here is his statement of purpose:

> I, the Teacher, was king over Israel in Jerusalem. I devoted myself to study and to explore by wisdom all that is done under heaven.
>
> —ECCLESIASTES 1:12–13

Solomon set his mind on the pursuit of wisdom and to understand the meaning behind everything God had made. As a king who reigned during peaceful times, he was able to devote himself entirely to this endeavor. It is interesting to note that this was his quest even after God appeared to Solomon in a dream:

> The Lord appeared to Solomon during the night in a dream, and God said, "Ask for whatever you want me to give you."
>
> —1 KINGS 3:5

Can you imagine the intensity of this moment? What if Solomon's heart had not been prepared?

I've said and done some pretty wild stuff in my dreams. He might have asked for a "good thing," yet missed the "God thing." He could have asked that Jerusalem would prosper and that his kingdom would expand. He could have asked for the health of his children and wives. But he did not.

Solomon's request was a reflection of what God desired in the king of Israel.

Solomon answered:

> Give your servant a discerning heart to govern your people and to distinguish between right and wrong. For who is able to govern this great people of yours?
> —1 Kings 3:9

This was not the answer of a know-it-all. Solomon was humbled by the gargantuan task set before him. The Lord was pleased with Solomon's response. So God blessed him with even more:

> Since you have asked for this and not for long life or wealth for yourself, nor have asked for the death of your enemies but for discernment in administering justice, I will do what you have asked. I will give you a wise and discerning heart, so that there will never have been anyone like you, nor will there ever be. Moreover, I will give you

21

what you have not asked for—both riches and honor—so that in your lifetime you will have no equal among kings.

—1 Kings 3:11–13

The Necessity of Wisdom

Not only would Solomon be the wisest man who had ever lived, but he would rise above his peers and his wisdom would outlive him to surpass the wisdom of all future generations of kings and leaders. With all our technology, computers and databases, Solomon was still wiser. He had none of these high-tech resources from which to draw. He drew from the counsel of the Creator.

Solomon was humbled by the gargantuan task set before him.

At first this claim might seem incredulous, but we can be certain it is indeed the truth because it was made by God. If we are awed by how this could possibly be true, it is because we are using a flawed measurement of wisdom.

There is a mistaken impression that the accumulation of knowledge is wisdom. If this were indeed true, to what lofty pinnacle has this vast knowledge brought us? We live in a culture brimming with excess, poverty, perversion, violence and wickedness. Ours is a generation of people who are self-ruled and haughty. Our world is riddled with disease, plague, want and war. It is obvious that in our pursuit of knowledge, we have forsaken truth.

Without wisdom we may possess all the knowledge this world may offer and still remain fools. It is not more technology or knowledge that we need. Our souls cry out for wisdom. Wisdom is the ability to apply knowledge, experience and truth while retaining proper relationship with God and man.

Wisdom gives us eyes to see and ears to hear. Only then will we recognize truth when we find it. In the pursuit of knowledge we have strayed from the path of wisdom and discretion. We have allowed knowledge to exalt us to the realm of self-rule. We have become a generation of self-ruled, self-motivated *fools*. "The fool says in his heart, 'There is no God'" (Ps. 14:1). We may acknowledge God's existence, while we live as though He did not.

> # Without wisdom we may possess all the knowledge this world may offer and still remain fools.

Solomon sensed his overwhelming need for wisdom. As ruler of God's people, he bore more than a national government upon his shoulders. He set his heart to make wisdom his lifelong pursuit. He held a royal position in which his riches were unfathomable, his influence worldwide, his authority and power respected and feared. Kings from all over the world brought tribute to Solomon in deference to his wisdom and excellence.

Solomon lived free from the fear of sudden death. God had promised him a long life, as long as he walked in His ways. It was in this boundless and prosperous atmosphere that Solomon expanded himself to experience, observe and encompass many facets of life.

In wisdom Solomon found true freedom from the worldly comparisons and judgments that could have kept him bound to his past. He learned to put aside the world's standard and to cast aside his fears. Fear can be a paralyzing force that keeps us bound to our past. In the next chapter we will learn to overcome the deceptive nature of fear.

Adapted from Lisa Bevere, *The True Measure of a Woman*, 22–36.

INNER BEAUTY TIP

LOVE CHALLENGES US
TO DOUBT WHAT WE CAN SEE
AND BELIEVE WHAT WE CANNOT.

2

Fear: The Battle for Your Mind

This is what the Lord says … "Fear not, for
I have redeemed you; I have summoned
you by name; you are mine."

—Isaiah 43:1

hy would anyone despise God's order in
their life? Why would they struggle to hold
on when they should let go? Why would they
want to retain and not relinquish control? Why?
Because they are afraid.

Fear is an insidious force. It causes reason and
wisdom to escape us. It drives and compels, push-
ing us to the brink of unbelief. To overcome fear

we must know its nature. Fear is not a mental state of mind or a bad attitude. It is a spirit.

> For God has not given us a spirit of fear, but of power and of love and of a sound mind.
>
> —2 TIMOTHY 1:7, NKJV

Fear is a spirit. It is not from God. It is sent by the enemy to torment our souls and defile our human spirits. Fear comes to steal our power, love and soundness of mind. As a spiritual force, fear must be confronted spiritually.

BATTLING FOR POWER

Fear is only empowered to the degree we yield to its deception. Fear steals our power by tricking us into believing its lies. Imaginary fears can become real if we believe in them. Even the most unfounded ones can alter the course of our lives and in turn change our destinies.

The destination for the children of Israel was the Promised Land, but they forsook God's promises to embrace their fears. They placed their faith in their fears. In doing this they chose the devil's lies over God's truth.

God said:

> I have come down to rescue them from the hand of the Egyptians and to bring them up out of that land into a good and spacious land, a land flowing with milk and honey...See, I am sending an angel ahead of you to guard you along the way and to bring you to the place I have prepared.
>
> —Exodus 3:8; 23:20

Fear said:

> "We can't attack those people; they are stronger than we are"...They spread among the Israelites a bad report...They said, "The land we explored devours those living in it. All the people we saw there are of great size ...We seemed like grasshoppers in our own eyes, and we looked the same to them."
>
> —Numbers 13:31–33

They believed:

> Why is the Lord bringing us to this land only to let us fall by the sword? Our wives and children will be taken as plunder. Wouldn't

it be better for us to go back to Egypt?
—NUMBERS 14:3

When they chose fear's lie over God's truth, they forfeited their power to possess the Promised Land God had already given them. Instead of inheriting the promises, they inherited their fears.

> As surely as I live, declares the LORD, I will do to you the very things I heard you say: In this desert your bodies will fall—every one of you twenty years old or more…who has grumbled against me. Not one of you will enter the land I swore with uplifted hand to make your home, except Caleb son of Jephunneh and Joshua son of Nun. As for your children that you said would be taken as plunder, I will bring them in to enjoy the land you have rejected…Your children will be shepherds here for forty years, suffering for your unfaithfulness, until the last of your bodies lies in the desert.
> —NUMBERS 14:28–33

God never planned for a generation of Israelites to die as they wandered the wilderness. His plan was to rescue them from the Egyptians and bring them, escorted by an angel, to a good land.

Instead of inheriting the promises, they inherited their fears.

Fear had so twisted and perverted their spiritual perception of God that the Israelites imagined God had tricked them. They believed He had delivered them from Egyptian oppression in order to turn them over to be slaughtered by the heathen nations of Canaan.

Their logic sounds ridiculous, doesn't it? Yet how often do we unknowingly succumb to the same sort of unreasonable fears? Fear causes us to shrink back into doubt and unbelief.

Fear is after our faith. It wants us to place our faith in it and not in the promise of God. Our faith will always work—but will it work *for* us or *against* us?

The Bible says that God gives each of us a measure of faith (Rom. 12:3). We are to be stewards of this faith. God wants us to use our faith to be conformed to the image of His Son. However, the enemy wants to use it against us and conform us to a different image. Don't turn the power of faith over to the enemy of God.

FIGHTING FOR LOVE

Fear is after your love because the enemy knows that love protects the believer from fear.

> God is love. Whoever lives in love lives in God, and God in him…There is no fear in love.
>
> —1 JOHN 4:16, 18

There is no greater protection afforded you than to live in God's love. It is here that you are hidden and inaccessible to the enemy.

There is no greater protection afforded you than to live in God's love.

The love of God drives out or cas
This description again confirms that fea,
itual force that must be dealt with spiritu,
are called to cast out spirits and deny our flesh. We
cannot deny a spirit and cast out our flesh, even
though some of us have tried.)

The very nature of love opposes the nature of
fear. Love's nature is described by the following
verses:

> Love is patient, love is kind. It does not
> envy, it does not boast, it is not proud. It is
> not rude, it is not self-seeking, it is not eas-
> ily angered, it keeps no record of wrongs.
> Love does not delight in evil but rejoices
> with the truth. It always protects, always
> trusts, always hopes, always perseveres.
>
> —1 CORINTHIANS 13:4–7

We can go through the above list and insert the
opposite attributes of fear. Fear is impatient,
mean, jealous, boastful, proud, rude, self-seeking
and easily angered. It keeps a record of wrongs. It
delights when the bad it predicted happens. It
never protects, trusts, hopes or perseveres.

33

Fear is the opposite of love. Love and fear both operate from belief in the unseen. Love challenges us to doubt what we see and believe what we cannot. Fear urges us to believe what is seen while doubting the unseen. Fear displaces love, and love casts out fear. Fear is the spiritual force that is in direct opposition to God's love and protection in our lives.

Jesus has already conquered the greatest fear any of us will face—the fear of death. As our High Priest He was moved with compassion by our weaknesses and understood not only the fear of death, but also all our fears. By victoriously facing our greatest fear (death), He conquered all lesser fears and their bondage.

> Since the children have flesh and blood, he too shared in their humanity so that by his death he might destroy him who holds the power of death—that is, the devil—and free those who all their lives were held in slavery by their fear of death.
>
> —Hebrews 2:14–15

Fear will hold you in slavery if you allow it to do so. Jesus triumphed over every grip of fear when

He laid down His life on the cross.

> Greater love has no one than this, that he lay down his life for his friends.
>
> —JOHN 15:13

Jesus laid down His life out of His love for us. Jesus conquered the fear that had mastered Adam. The fear of death had ruled since Adam's transgression in the garden. It was Adam's desire to be like God that caused him to transgress.

Jesus triumphed over every grip of fear when He laid down His life on the cross.

FEAR IN THE GARDEN

God carefully warned Adam when He commanded the man:

> You must not eat from the tree of the knowledge of good and evil, for when you eat of it you will surely die.
>
> —GENESIS 2:17

The knowledge of good and evil is the law of sin and death. God wanted Adam to remain in the liberty of His knowledge of God. Adam had gained this knowledge by loving and fellowshiping with God. He did not need the knowledge of good and evil to walk with God. Adam was already walking with God. Satan did not want Adam and Eve to remain free and alive under this law of liberty, so he perverted God's warning of protection.

> "You will not surely die," the serpent said to the woman. "For God knows that when you eat of it your eyes will be opened, and you will be like God, knowing good and evil."
> —GENESIS 3:4–5

Adam knew God was life, and in Him there was no darkness or death. Satan made it sound as though God were intentionally deceiving Adam to prevent him from becoming like God. What Satan did was twofold: First, He undermined God by questioning His truthfulness and motives; second, He appealed to Adam's desire to be like God but not subject to Him. His underlying message was, "Why should you believe and obey God? He doesn't have your best interests in mind. Be the lord of yourself."

Adam and Eve believed this deception. They ate the fruit hoping it would provide the wisdom necessary to be their own masters. They reasoned that the more they were like God, the less they would be subject to Him.

But were they now *more* like God? Let's examine Adam's first reply to God after eating the fruit.

> I heard you in the garden, and I was afraid because I was naked; so I hid.
>
> —GENESIS 3:10

If Adam and Eve had become more like God, why were they afraid of Him, hiding from His presence?

The fear of judgment will always come between you and the presence of God.

Fear distorted Adam's perception of God. He

became afraid of the very One who formed and breathed life into him. Adam feared his Creator because he had transgressed God's command.

Perfect love and fear cannot abide together, so Adam had to leave the garden of God. The fear of judgment will always come between you and the presence of God.

Adam's transgression brought him under the law of sin and death. Adam chose the knowledge of good and evil (the law) over the knowledge of God (a love relationship by the Spirit). Adam wanted to be like God apart from God. Adam grasped for equality with God.

The second Adam, Jesus, was God and became man. He is our example:

> Your attitude should be the same as that of Christ Jesus: Who, being in very nature God, did not consider equality with God something to be grasped...he humbled himself and became obedient to death— even death on a cross!
>
> —Philippians 2:5–6, 8

Jesus lived His life under the rule and dominion

of God His Father. He was not self-ruled. He refused to move independently of God. He thrived on obeying God (John 4:34). Through obedience Jesus reversed the law of sin and death and its dominion of fear.

> Through Christ Jesus the law of the Spirit of life set me free from the law of sin and death.
>
> —ROMANS 8:2

We are therefore governed by the Spirit and not by the law. Fear cannot wage its war in a heart submitted to and directed by the love of God.

Now let's go on to why fear attacks your soundness of mind.

A SOUND MIND

Since fear is a spiritual force without form, it must inhabit something to gain expression. It seeks to inhabit the fortresses of the mind. The battle of fear is waged in our minds.

One of Satan's battle strategies is to torment us with questions. Satan questioned Eve as to whether God really meant what He had said. He was trying to undermine God and make Him look like a liar.

Fear behaves the same way. It always questions, distorts and undermines what God has said. *How do you know God will do what He said? Maybe you misunderstood Him. God really meant this? That promise does not apply to you.*

Fear always questions, distorts and undermines what God has said.

Fear wants you to compromise the integrity of the Word of God. God has exalted His Word above His name (Ps. 138:2, NKJV). When we doubt His Word, we doubt all that He is. Fear wants us to doubt God's goodness, mercy, faithfulness, holiness, power, glory and everything else that makes Him God. Fear will try to misrepresent the nature and motive of God by twisting His Word. This will cause us to doubt God, and we do not trust or believe those we doubt.

Fear wants to convince us that God did not mean what He said or say what He meant. By undermining God's character and distorting His words, fear brings in confusion to torment us. Confusion attacks the soundness, or wholeness, of our minds.

Confusion divides our allegiance between God and self. This leaves us with a double mind. James 1:6–8 accurately describes this confusion:

> But when he asks, he must believe and not doubt, because he who doubts is like a wave of the sea, blown and tossed by the wind. That man should not think he will receive anything from the Lord; he is a double-minded man, unstable in all he does.

When we are confused we are unstable. Instability causes a person to waver and shift—not just in one area but in all he does. James said that if we doubt, we shouldn't think we'll receive anything from the Lord. James made this comment while asking for wisdom. So when we lose soundness or wholeness of mind, we lose the guidance of God. Uncertainty takes over. We don't know what to expect from God, so we take matters into our own hands.

Fear mocks, *What will happen if you let go? Who will watch out for you?* Fear has torment (1 John 4:18, NKJV) because it leads us to question, *What is going to happen to me?* Such questioning diverts your attention from God and back to yourself. Fear encourages us to safeguard our well-being. It wants us to preserve ourselves.

Self-preservation requires us to be self-centered, self-serving, selfish, self-willed and self-ruled. These attributes directly oppose God's directives for our lives and thus remove God's protection. The enemy wants us to serve in the kingdom of self. In this kingdom self rules; therefore self is our god.

> *Self*-preservation requires
> us to be self-centered,
> self-serving, selfish,
> self-willed and self-ruled.

Fight Back

Now that we've seen how fear attacks in the arenas of power, love and soundness of mind, let's look at how we can fight back against the strongholds of fear.

Author Francis Frangipane describes a stronghold in our mind as a "house of thoughts." Strongholds of fear are often constructed from the lies of the enemy and from debris left over from past hurt and abuse. These materials from past offenses are collected and used to construct walls to protect us from those we fear will hurt us. Fear instead of faith establishes the thought patterns through which all information is processed. Every thought is conformed to the image of fear and unbelief.

Our reasoning is distorted, and our soundness of mind is disturbed. This explains how we can say something to a person tormented by fear and that person will hear something entirely different. The words are heard, but the meaning is distorted. That is why God could say, "You will be ever hearing but never understanding" (Acts 28:26). They heard, but because of unbelief they could not perceive or understand the meaning of what they heard.

> The weapons we fight with are not the weapons of the world. On the contrary, they have divine power to demolish strongholds. We demolish arguments and every pretension that sets itself up against the knowledge of God, and we take captive every thought to make it obedient to Christ.
>
> —2 CORINTHIANS 10:4–5

God wants these strongholds demolished. Notice these arguments and pretensions set themselves up against or in opposition to the knowledge of God. Remember, the battle is in our minds. The enemy wants to set self in opposition to the knowledge of God. To combat this, God wants every thought that wars against our minds to be taken hostage and conformed to the image of Christ. That means we are to capture the messages of fear and unbelief and subject them to the truth of God's Word. Jesus is the Word made flesh, so when we subject our thoughts to the Word we are subjecting them to Christ (John 1:1–3, 14).

God wants every thought that wars against our minds to be taken hostage and conformed to the image of Christ.

We are not to make our thoughts obedient to the Law. The Bible tells us that we are to make them obedient to Christ. The Law has no power to tear down these strongholds. In fact, it helps with their construction.

> Once I was alive apart from law; but when the commandment came, sin sprang to life and I died. I found that the very commandment that was intended to bring life actually brought death. For sin, seizing the opportunity afforded by the commandment, deceived me, and through the commandment put me to death.
>
> —ROMANS 7:9–11

For what the law was powerless to do in

45

that it was weakened by the sinful nature, God did by sending his own Son in the likeness of sinful man to be a sin offering. And so he condemned sin in sinful man…For you did not receive a spirit that makes you a slave again to fear, but you received the Spirit of sonship. And by him we cry, "Abba, Father."

—Romans 8:3, 15

We died to the rule of the law of sin and death when we were crucified with Christ. At that point we received the spirit of sonship. Instead of self ruling us, Christ became our king. Therefore we are subject to Him.

Under the Law we were created in the image of our natural father Adam. But in the new and living law of life in Christ Jesus we are granted sonship with our Father God.

Renew Your Mind

Because we are under an aggressive onslaught from the enemy, we must also be aggressive in the protection of our minds. We must guard them diligently. This is accomplished by renewing our minds through the Word of God.

> Do not conform any longer to the pattern of this world, but be transformed by the renewing of your mind. Then you will be able to test and approve what God's will is—his good, pleasing and perfect will.
> —Romans 12:2

Fear always casts doubt on our knowing the will of God, but we can know God's will through the transformation of our minds. If we are able to know His good, pleasing and perfect will, we will not be afraid to submit to it.

> The mind of sinful man is death, but the mind controlled by the Spirit is life and peace.
> —Romans 8:6

God wants our minds controlled by His Spirit, not by the spirit of fear. Fear will keep us in constant restlessness and confusion. It does not want us to experience peace. Notice that the sinful, unbelieving mind leads to death, while God's Spirit leads us to the path of life and peace.

> You will keep in perfect peace him whose

mind is steadfast, because he trusts in you.
—ISAIAH 26:3

God will do this because we trust Him and choose to believe that He meant what He said. We experience peace when we choose His faithfulness over fear.

> Because we are under an aggressive onslaught from the enemy, we must also be aggressive in the protection of our minds.

Renewing our minds is more than just a knowledge of the Scriptures. It is trusting His goodness and faithfulness even when we don't understand how His Word will be accomplished in our lives. By believing what we don't see and understand, we mix His Word with faith. This is the only way God's Word becomes alive in us.

For we also have had the gospel preached to

us, just as they did; but the message they heard was of no value to them, because those who heard did not combine it with faith.

—HEBREWS 4:2

The knowledge of the gospel was of no value to the children of Israel wandering in the wilderness even though they were accompanied day and night by His presence, a cloud by day and a pillar of fire by night. We are warned that the same can happen to us if we are not careful.

To inherit God's promise of eternal life, Jesus instructed:

Love the Lord your God with all your heart and with all your soul and with all your mind.

—MATTHEW 22:37

Adapted from *Out of Control and Loving It!*, 105–117.

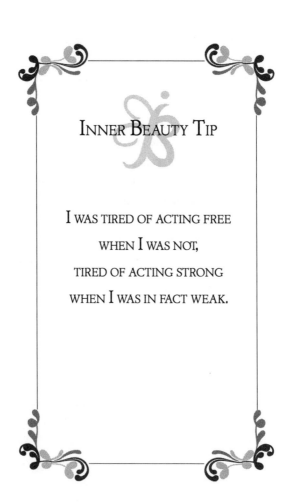

INNER BEAUTY TIP

I WAS TIRED OF ACTING FREE
WHEN I WAS NOT,
TIRED OF ACTING STRONG
WHEN I WAS IN FACT WEAK.

3

Awake, Daughter of Zion

Awake, awake, O Zion, clothe yourself with
strength. Put on your garments of splendor,
O Jerusalem, the holy city. The uncircumcised and defiled will not enter you again.
Shake off your dust; rise up, sit enthroned,
O Jerusalem. Free yourself from the chains
on your neck, O captive Daughter of Zion.

—Isaiah 52:1–2

begin this chapter with this scripture because
I believe hidden within its poignant imagery
is a wealth of truth. These truths began an
awakening in my life, one that resonated through
my soul until my entire being was touched. I share
its precious message of freedom with you. I invite
you to ponder and dissect it with me, searching
each segment for its hidden truth. Together let's

51

visit this captive daughter of Zion.

I envision her hopelessly chained to a wall of stone. I see the footprints in the dusty earth where she struggled to escape. Her neck is rubbed raw where the metal yoke encircles it. She mindlessly paces the length of her chain, retracing each step, in search of some key to set her free. She scans the dust, poking and probing each crevice in the wall.

Hopeless and discouraged she now sits in the dust, shoulders bent, clothes ragged, strength spent. Though it is day, she lapses into an exhausted stupor of restless sleep.

Then I see a strong messenger arrive. I watch over his shoulder as he pities this worn and wounded woman. He stands before her, silently watching as her head tosses in her sleep. Suddenly he steps forward, shakes her and calls her by name.

> Awake, awake, O Zion, clothe yourself with strength. Put on your garments of splendor …Shake off your dust; rise up, sit enthroned, O Jerusalem. Free yourself from the chains on your neck, O captive Daughter of Zion.

She struggles to her feet, swaying weakly and pointing to the wall, the chain and her yoke. "Help me," she pleads as she strains for his hand, but he steps back beyond her reach.

"Shake off your dust; rise up, sit enthroned, O Jerusalem. Free yourself from the chains on your neck, O captive Daughter of Zion."

Once again he repeats his message, pauses, turns and walks away.

Bewildered she calls after him, but the wind snatches her voice, and he does not return. She laments, "The wall is too solid; my chain, too heavy; and I, too weak to lift myself out from all this!" In despair she strains at her chain until she no longer can stand the pressure of resisting. She moves back to the shelter of her wall. At least there she can feel what is behind her and see what is in front of her.

I rehearsed this scenario over and over in my mind, acutely feeling her pain and frustration. Why was my vision so clear? It was because I too was a captive daughter of Zion.

It is a contradiction for a daughter of Zion to be captive. A daughter is an heir, and a daughter of Zion is an heir of God! How could any child of God be held captive? Yet it was true that I was bound.

I would comfort myself, thinking, *Perhaps if I attend this seminar or if that person prays for me I'll be free.* So with each new teaching or sermon I'd back up, then run, endeavoring to break loose, declaring, "This time I've had enough!" But my chain was too strong, and its length always yanked me back to the bitter reality of my bondage.

Tired of constant disappointment I resigned myself to my condition. I decided it was better not to hope than to hope and only be disappointed again. So I concealed my chains and quietly moved within the confines of my restrictions.

Then the Holy Spirit blew the words of Isaiah 52:1–2 my way. They intrigued me with their vivid imagery and contrast. I drew a parallel between this ancient prisoner and myself.

I was tired of acting free when I was not, tired of acting strong when I was in fact weak. I hungered more for freedom than I cared for the approval of those around me. I had already discovered that their approval could never set me free.

So began my quest. No man, woman or ministry could ever set me free. My freedom lay hidden somewhere in this message from my Father, my Maker.

In my mind I visited this captive daughter of Zion many times. Each time she looked a little worse and more hopeless than the last. The last time I saw her she sat numbly in the dust as the messenger spoke to her.

She lifted her head only slightly as she silently watched him walk away. It seemed the sun was setting on her hope for freedom. Who was this messenger? Had her enemy sent him to taunt her with dreams that would never come true?

But this time as the stranger mounted the hill that would once again take him from her sight, he turned and looked back.

Puzzled, she scanned his outline against the setting sun. The wind carried his words to her ears again: "Awake, awake, O Zion…"

But this time the voice was different. She recognized who was calling her. It was the voice of one she loved long ago. Deep within she sensed a strange strength. What if she dared to hear and grasp the meaning of these words?

He knew who she was. Now she knew Him as well: It was her Father calling to her.

She lifted her head and met his gaze. Though he was far off she heard the message clearly, "Free yourself from the chains on your neck, O captive Daughter of Zion." He knew who she was. Now she knew Him as well: It was her Father calling to her. This messenger was sent by Him!

I believe this picture illustrates the condition of the majority of women in the body of Christ. Heirs…yet captive. Free…yet bound.

What did this poignant daughter see? How did she come to herself and realize her freedom?

I believe this book holds such a journey for you. I believe you have it in your hands for a reason and a purpose. This message will set free the daughters of Zion yet to be revealed, a generation awaiting their release. I see them lifting their heads, listening for the wind of the Holy Spirit.

I pray that through these truths you will find your freedom and realize your destiny. You may doubt me, but dare to believe your Father God.

Adapted from *Out of Control and Loving It!*, 19–22.

INNER BEAUTY TIP

THE MOST DESOLATE OF
WASTELANDS IS OUR PAST.
IT HOLDS NO LIFE,
AND ITS ARID SOIL
IS INSATIABLE.

4

Rise Up From the Dust

So much transpires in Isaiah 52:1–2 that I feel it is necessary to point out each step of God's process. Therefore we will examine it point by point, process by process. Let's go deeper and look closer at this woman and the message.

—AN URGENT SUMMONS

 wake, awake, O Zion…" It is important to note that the messenger repeats himself. This accomplished two purposes:

- It awakened her from her slumber.
- It alerted her to her true condition.

The words snapped her from the sleep that shrouded her, pulling her from the dream in which she was hidden. She was trapped by her past yet afraid of her future. Stepping forward while always looking back.

Most mornings when I awaken my children for school, I try to be pleasant, saying in a singsong voice, "Time to get up." I enjoy watching them stretch and turn their sleepy faces toward me as they blink at the morning light. I may even gently motivate them to move a little faster with, "Daddy's making pancakes." They smile and tumble from their bunks. The morning process has begun.

Then there are other mornings—the ones when we've overslept. My wake-up style is altogether different on those days. I storm into their rooms, flip on the light and command, "Wake up!" Once I know they can hear me, I inform them of the lateness of the hour and the urgency of the moment. "You're being picked up in fifteen minutes!" Their eyes pop open as they snap into action. There is no time for pancakes on these mornings. Everything is a push to get them out the door on time.

I remember being awakened in this manner when I was young. It was never pleasant. But it was far worse to wake up and realize you had already missed your ride. In one case you have a chance to beat the clock, but in the other the clock has already beaten you.

By sounding the wake-up call twice, I believe the messenger was saying, "Wake up! It is very late, and you are in danger of remaining captive!"

But this daughter of Zion was sleepy with oppression and depression. Withdrawn and alone. Restrained and weary. She wondered if she would ever be free.

He knew who she was even though she thought she had been forgotten.

Notice the messenger called her by name, *O Zion.* He wanted her to know for certain that he was speaking directly to her. This was not a general alarm but a specific mandate. He knew who she was even though she thought she had been forgotten.

Get Dressed

He recognized her weakness and said, "Clothe yourself with strength." He did not offer to strengthen her, but he told her to strengthen herself. I'm sure she thought, *I have no strength.* When we come to the end of our own strength, we find God's strength. A captive prisoner has no natural strength to speak of. That was not the kind she needed. She needed inner strength, the type only God supplies. She needed to draw from His well of water, the source of strength deep inside, the spring that never fails. She lifted her head.

Pointing to the clothes that had been stripped from her, the messenger urged, "Put on your garments of splendor." I believe these garments represent her crushed hopes and discarded dreams, those dreams that constant disappointment and abuse snatched from her. This messenger thrust them back into her hands. She marveled that they had been kept safe and intact. She had feared she would never see them again. Clutching them in her hand she thought, *Do I dare? I failed when I was younger and stronger. I've been unfaithful. Are these still mine?*

62

The messenger sensed her fear and reassured her in more intimate terms, "O Jerusalem, the holy city. The uncircumcised and defiled will not enter you again."

With this he told her, "I know who you are, what you have done and what has happened to you." Then he addressed her fear of failure and recurring harassment. He assured her that no longer would she be raped, defiled and robbed of her dignity. She was holy, renewed and protected.

Zion represents all that is of Jewish descent. This includes the natural seed of Abraham, which is the nation of Israel, and the spiritual seed of Abraham, which is the church. The word *Jerusalem* in this passage points to the holy city "prepared as a bride beautifully dressed for her husband" (Rev. 21:2). The messenger spoke affectionately to restore her, calling her forth as a remnant of the whole.

Shake It Off

"Shake off your dust" signifies an aggressive removal of all that had dirtied or soiled her. The dust is the remains of past journeys and failures.

63

Dust is carried in by the wind, but it accumulates in vacant stillness. It settles on barren ground void of vegetation and moisture, producing lands of famine. The most desolate of these wastelands is our past. It holds no life; its arid soil is insatiable, draining our very life.

This desperate woman sat surrounded by dust. Each new wind blew more her way—the dust of past wounds and failures. The longer we sit in our past and the more we study it, the more we are doomed to repeat it. We must shake it off.

> The most desolate of these wastelands is our past. It holds no life; its arid soil is insatiable, draining our very life.

The daughter of Zion brushed the dust from her shoulders and arms. She wiped it from her eyes and tossed it out of her hair.

Rise Up and Take Your Place

The messenger told her, "Rise up." She stood and left her past on the ground.

She was then told, "Sit enthroned, O Jerusalem."

The beloved of God is no longer to sit in her past mistakes, abuses and failures. A throne has been prepared for her. A position of delegated authority awaits her. She is to rest in this position, exercising and enjoying the rights and privileges it provides. This throne is for God's children, the broken and contrite.

Having delivered these pledges and promises the messenger exclaimed, "Free yourself from the chains on your neck, O captive daughter of Zion."

He acknowledged that she was indeed captive, but he let her know she did not have to remain that way. He assured her that it was within her power to free herself from the chains of bondage.

The chains did not bind her hands or feet, nor did they encircle her waist. They encompassed and immobilized her neck. Even though she could fully move her arms and legs, she was tethered and restricted by the neck.

She moved cautiously, aware of her limits. Yet she was spurred on by the hope of freedom she began to feel for what she could not see. When she had shaken herself and brushed the dust from her garments, she thought she felt something.

The key to freedom is already hidden in the hearts of those who dare to believe.

So she lifted the collar of her tattered rags and reached toward her heart. Her chains had kept her from seeing it, but her finger could trace the outline of a key resting against her bosom. She pulled it out into the fading sunlight and turned it over in her hand. She had never seen the lock that sealed the yoke around her neck. All she could do was feel it. But she was certain this must be the key. Her Father had hidden it here for just such a time. She inserted the key into the lock, and with a rusty groan her chains fell at her feet.

So many of us are leashed to a wall. We move

our arms and legs, but our activity takes us nowhere. We're held captive by the throat.

The key to freedom is already hidden in the hearts of those who dare to believe. It is not the key to something…but to Someone.

> Behold, I stand at the door and knock.
> —REVELATION 3:20, NKJV

It is up to us to use the key and unlock the door of our captive hearts.

Adapted from *Out of Control and Loving It!*, 25–29.

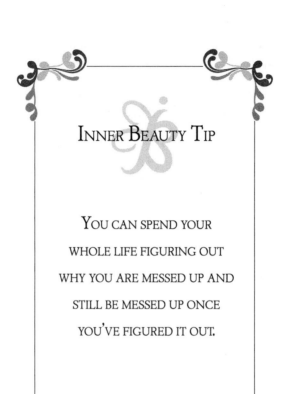

INNER BEAUTY TIP

YOU CAN SPEND YOUR
WHOLE LIFE FIGURING OUT
WHY YOU ARE MESSED UP AND
STILL BE MESSED UP ONCE
YOU'VE FIGURED IT OUT.

5

Your Past Is Not Your Future

Forget the former things; do not dwell on the past. See, I am doing a new thing! Now it springs up; do you not perceive it?
—Isaiah 43:18–19

Perhaps you have felt bound by your own pain, frustration and broken dreams. You may have been angered and frustrated by messages of liberty that only cause you to feel more bound. Maybe you have groped for the hand of your deliverer, hoping for assistance or support, but find that his hand was just beyond your reach. Though you struggled to be released from the chains that bind you, eventually you settled back down into the dust of your past.

Your past is not your future.

When you have come to an end of yourself you are ripe—no, desperate—for change. You may even now be saying, "I've tried so many times, and it has never worked!" I have a word from God for you: *Your past is not your future.*

If we measure our future by our past, we are doomed to repeat it. It is a fallacy to believe that by studying our past failures, traumas or abuses we prevent or correct our current ones. Looking at our past does not guarantee our future—it prevents it. When we search, analyze and delve into our yesterdays, we are limited to our own accumulated information of abuse or wrong decisions. Drawing on our own wisdom and experience will not safeguard our future.

We need someone bigger and wiser than ourselves to guide and protect us—we need God. He knows the end from the beginning. He sees the whole picture clearly, while we see only a fragment dimly and distorted (1 Cor. 13:12). He is independent of time while we are subject to it. How can we draw on this wisdom?

First, we must treat our past the way God prescribes. So how does God process our past? What is His instruction?

Your Past Is Gone

> Brothers, I do not consider myself yet to have taken hold of it. But one thing I do: Forgetting what is behind and straining toward what is ahead, I press on toward the goal to win the prize for which God has called me heavenward in Christ Jesus.
>
> —Philippians 3:13–14

One day the Holy Spirit spoke to me, contrasting this verse with what appears to be its present-day application. He warned, "The church is straining for what is behind and forgetting what is ahead."

When we stretch back and try to make sense of all that happened in the past, we are bound to be frustrated. Constantly replaying, reviewing and rewinding, we build different scenarios of what might have been. It's like trying to walk forward while looking backward. We think, *If only I had done this or that, things would have been different.* Yes, it is true; things would have been different. But you didn't do it differently, and thinking about it *now* can't change it *then.* Your past, no matter how tragic or terrible, is gone. You can never reach back into it and change it.

Even the wonderful parts of your past are gone. Don't try to live in them and allow them to drain your life in the present. It will only waste your time and energy.

God never goes back, although He is the only one who can. He goes forward. He is always looking ahead and moving beyond the present.

When Adam fell, God did not sit down and think, *Where did I go wrong? I never should have planted that tree! I should have set up an angel to guard it. Now I'm going to have to start over. I'd better figure this out so it won't happen again.*

No, God explained to Adam and Eve the immediate and far-reaching consequences of their actions. Yet even in the midst of this sad separation He prophesied their redemption from the Fall and the curse of sin (Gen. 3:15).

> # God is always looking ahead and moving beyond the present.

This is a tragic truth: You can spend your whole life figuring out why you are messed up and still be messed up once you've figured it out. After all your searching you know the *why*. But knowing the why does not produce the power to change. You must know the *Who*. You don't go to the problem for the answer. You must move from the problem to the answer. Our answer is Jesus. The question is, Do we believe what He did was enough?

Too often we allow the enemy to deceive us into believing our case is unique or our hurt is too big for God. We think, *I'm a special exception and therefore need to be handled differently.* So we gather all the information and tell our story, trying to discover why something happened. Unfortunately, knowing why doesn't necessarily mean we will ever make sense of what happened.

FORGET IT

> Awake, awake, O Zion, clothe yourself with strength. Put on your garments of splendor, O Jerusalem, the holy city. The uncircumcised and defiled will not enter you again. Shake off your dust; rise up, sit enthroned, O Jerusalem. Free yourself from the chains on your neck, O captive Daughter of Zion.
> —ISAIAH 52:1–2

Our friend, the woman in Isaiah 52:1–2, represents Israel when she was taken into captivity for forgetting God. The people had committed all types of idolatry, had broken every commandment He gave and were proud and haughty. (See Isaiah 1.)

In this captivity the Israelites felt hopeless and forlorn. They were afraid God would leave them in their bondage. Their guilt weighed so heavily upon them that they doubted God could ever forgive their iniquity. As they looked around at the Babylonian citizens and the strange land of captivity, all they could do was remember what had been. Their failures were ever before them.

God did not say, "I want you to remember your shame and learn from it." He said, "Forget about it because I have."

But when God spoke to them during this captivity He comforted them and painted a very different picture—one of hope. He wanted them to stir themselves to believe He would once again restore them. He told them to forget their past failures and unfaithfulness.

> Do not be afraid; you will not suffer shame. Do not fear disgrace; you will not be humiliated. You will forget the shame of your youth and remember no more the reproach of your widowhood.
>
> —Isaiah 54:4

God did not say, "I want you to remember your shame and learn from it." He said, "Forget about it because I have." He addressed their fears, admonishing them, "Don't be afraid. I won't let you be shamed, disgraced or humiliated. I won't not remind you of your past, so don't let anyone else— forget about it." In essence God was saying, "You once were that; now I have made you new; soon you'll be this!"

MORE THAN WE EXPECT

> See, I am doing a new thing! Now it springs
> up; do you not perceive it? I am making a
> way in the desert and streams in the waste-
> land.
>
> —ISAIAH 43:19

God enjoys turning our wastelands into fertile plains. He has a plan for irrigating our arid land. He knows this plan; we do not.

Those who look back say, "Tomorrow will be like today, because today was like yesterday." This is not how God views things. He understands that our human nature battles fear, so He encourages us.

> "For I know the plans I have for you,"
> declares the Lord, "plans to prosper you
> and not to harm you, plans to give you
> hope and a future."
>
> —Jeremiah 29:11

Notice that God does not outline the plan, nor does He say, "You will know the plan." He only assures us He knows the plan, and it is good.

God enjoys turning our wastelands into fertile plains.

Of course we would like to hear the details. We want to know when, where, how and with whom. I have a theory that even if He told us all these specific details we still would ask why. So He gives no specifics and affords us the opportunity to trust Him.

We feel overwhelmed if we try to figure out all of these elements. We can't. We don't have the necessary information. Even when we think we've figured out the plan, God never does what we expect. In reality, He does more.

> Now to him who is able to do immeasurably more than all we ask or imagine, according to his power that is at work within us.
>
> —EPHESIANS 3:20

Dare to believe when you cannot see or understand. Decide to trust God instead of dwelling on your fears. This is the powerful force that separates the believers from the unbelievers. Complete knowledge does not require faith. God challenges us simply to trust Him and His Word.

My husband, John, always shares this truth: "Only one person can get you out of the will of God—you!" No man, woman, minister, ministry, parent, spouse or friend can do it. Only you. When you set yourself in agreement with God's will and plan for your life, the opinions of men, women, organizations and devils no longer matter. It does not matter how many times those around you have failed. It does not matter how many times you've failed. God never has.

If God is for you, who can be against you (Rom. 8:31)? God's purpose will prevail—unless, of course, you choose not to believe.

If no one can get you out of God's will, then it is equally certain that only you can move into it. It is a decision you make on your own.

THE CHOICE IS YOURS

The most striking point of Isaiah 52 is that the woman's freedom utterly depended upon *her* taking action, not God. It was her response to God's directive that determined her destiny. God had already supplied everything she needed to attain her freedom, but she had to act on the message. It had to be mixed with faith. It was now her choice—to believe or remain bound.

> It was her response to God's directive that determined her destiny.

Often we make others responsible. We want

them to help us. We look to family, friends or ministries, thinking that if we just could get close enough to them we would be free. But usually the closer we get, the more flaws we see. We then realize they too are only human and must depend upon God. They tumble off pedestals upon which they never should have been placed. Their demise often leaves us feeling disillusioned.

God allows this for a reason. He wants us to look at the message, not the messenger. He wants to receive all the glory for what He does in our lives. We are granted the privilege of laboring with Him in this process. He trains our hands for war and our fingers for battle (Ps. 144:1).

When we set our hearts to pursue God and all that He has provided, all hell trembles. It is then that the enemy releases his onslaught of discouragement. Constantly trying to turn us back, he points to our past failures and fears. Discouraged, we often mistake the enemy's resistance as God's refusal to help us.

God is not refusing; He is waiting on us. Decide today that you will no longer tolerate captivity. Do not live in less than what Jesus' death provided.

You are to reign with Him. Choose His life.

I felt impressed to close this chapter with this word of encouragement from my journal. These words were specific to me, but I also give Scripture references so you can see how they apply to you. God never contradicts His Word. This is something the Lord gave to me in prayer. Let it minister hope to you.

JOURNAL EXCERPT

I know you feel empty and dry, My child, and this emptying is of Me. I am removing the last of the old, but do not move to the soul. Stay in the spirit. Spring up, O well! Call that well forth. Ask Me for rain. Call out for My refreshing. You are on the threshold and in need of My strength to put you over. Worship and praise before Me. Let your mind be still. This will be your strength and refreshing.

Do not plan out or premeditate, but know that I will cause those who have risen up against you to be ashamed and confounded before you. Only do not be afraid or allow terror to creep in as before, but gird yourself with love and praise. Guard what you hear and say, for the enemy longs to sow tares of strife. Be of few words, for you will have little to say until I fill your mouth, but soon you will break forth in an overflow.[1]

Before you go any further, boldly pray this with me:

This day I make a decision to fear and honor You, God, above all my past failures and over all that would seek to discourage or distract me.

Adapted from *Out of Control and Loving It!*, 31–38.

---

1. Scriptures related to the journal excerpt: Numbers 21:17; Psalm 35:4; 138:2; 141:3; Isaiah 52:9; Jeremiah 1:17–19; Matthew 13:36–43; John 4:13–14; 1 John 4:18.

Conclusion

At times it can be more comfortable to remain bound to our pasts than to rid our lives of these hindering bondages and reveal the inner beauty within. But we must become free of our pasts to step into the beauty of a woman of God.

In the Old Testament we have an example from the life of Hezekiah that can help us recognize the importance of tearing down our past and freeing our lives of those things that once dominated us—the "high places" that hinder God's beauty from shining forth:

> [Hezekiah] did what was right in the eyes of the LORD, just as his father David had done. He removed the high places, smashed the sacred stones and cut down the Asherah poles. He broke into pieces the bronze snake Moses had made, for up to that time the

Israelites had been burning incense to it.
                                        —2 KINGS 18:3–4

Hezekiah served God with all his heart just as David had done. He was valiant for the Lord. He tore down the idols of the people, even the one serpent Moses had fashioned. He recognized people had idolized even what God had done. I'm sure he was not necessarily popular with the people for his position, but he was popular with God.

> Hezekiah trusted in the LORD, the God of Israel. There was no one like him among all the kings of Judah, either before him or after him. He held fast to the LORD and did not cease to follow him; he kept the commands the LORD had given Moses. And the LORD was with him; he was successful in whatever he undertook.
>
> —2 KINGS 18:5–7

When we don't tear down the high places, we find ourselves again serving and paying tribute to idolatry. You may question, "Am I a leader? Am I not a mere woman? What could I do? How could I possibly tear down any high places?"

Have you not repented? Do you not have sight? Have you not been given authority, power and position?

Not only is a kingly anointing on your life, but there is also a priestly anointing. Now tear down the high places. Begin in your own life with the high hindering walls of your past that block God's glory from shining forth in your life. Then use the radiant fire of your inner beauty to encourage others to do the same. Though you may not possess authority in a natural earthly kingdom, you do in the heavenlies. You have the delegated authority of the Son of God; you have His Word; you have been washed in His blood; and He has all glory and dominion forever!

You have been granted a view high above all this present deception and darkness. Your eyes have been enlightened by the Truth to the truth—and it has set you free. Refuse to pay homage, tribute or honor to idols any longer. Stand strong and do not be entangled again with the yoke of slavery.

> It is for freedom that Christ has set us free.
> Stand firm, then, and do not let yourselves

be burdened again by a yoke of slavery.

—GALATIANS 5:1

You can escape your past. You can rise far above any hindering influences—any high places—that deter you from allowing your inner beauty to shine forth in a dark world. You can be the woman of God He wants you to be.

Adapted from Lisa Bevere, *You Are Not What You Weigh*, 139–141.

If you are enjoying the Inner Beauty Series by Lisa Bevere, here are some other titles from Charisma House that we think will minister to you...

Out of Control and Loving It!
Lisa Bevere
ISBN: 0-88419-436-1
Retail Price: $12.99

Lisa Bevere's life was a whirlwind of turmoil until she discovered that whenever she was in charge, things ended up in a mess. *Out of Control and Loving It!* is her journey from fearful, frantic control to a haven of rest and peace under God's control.

You Are Not What You Weigh
Lisa Bevere
ISBN: 0-88419-661-5
Retail Price: $10.99

Are you tired of reading trendy diet books, taking faddish pills and ordering the latest in infomercial exercise equipment? This is not another "how-to-lose-weight" book. Dare to believe, and this will be the last book you'll need to finally end your war with food and break free from the bondage of weight watching.

The True Measure of a Woman
Lisa Bevere
ISBN: 0-88419-487-6
Retail Price: $11.99

In her frank, yet gentle manner, Lisa Bevere exposes the subtle influences and blatant lies that hold many women captive. With the unveiling truth of God's Word, she displaces these lies and helps you discover who you are in Christ.

 To pick up a copy of any of these titles, contact your local Christian bookstore or order online at www.charismawarehouse.com.